THE STORY OF HOPE

Helping Kids Express Feelings of Grief and Loss

ASHLIN GRACE GORDON
and Melinda Gordon

Published by Redemption Press, PO Box 427, Enumclaw, WA 98022

Toll Free (844) 2REDEEM (273-3336)

Redemption Press is honored to present this title in partnership with the author. The views expressed or implied in this work are those of the author. Redemption Press provides our imprint seal representing design excellence, creative content, and high quality production.

ISBN: 978-1-68314-149-5

978-1-68314-154-9 (epub)

978-1-68314-155-6 (mobi)

Library of Congress Catalog Card Number: 2016953354

DEDICATION

To Abby and Simon, with all the love our hearts can hold.

DEAR PARENTS AND CAREGIVERS,

As you know, personalities differ with each child and each handles difficult situations in his or her own unique way. Grief is no different. Death is a hard reality for children to process, oftentimes more so when they see their parents and loved ones in pain.

My daughter Ashlin is a quiet, reflective, and observant child who does not always speak her feelings or show her emotions freely. As my husband and I grieved the loss of our youngest daughter, we were intentional in keeping a close eye on Ashlin as she, too, grieved. One morning, a few weeks after Abby died, I asked Ashlin how she was doing. She gave me a quick shrug of her shoulder, as if to brush me off. So I grabbed a legal pad, drew a few facial expressions, and asked her to circle the picture that matched how she felt. She did. The next morning, I did the same. Within no time, Ashlin no longer needed pictures or drawings or promptings to express her emotions. This method became a turning point in Ashlin's healing because she learned to express how she felt, not simply with a shrug of the shoulder, but through pictures.

Grief support is often focused on the parents, offering little to siblings. We want to change this by giving brothers and sisters a safe outlet to express their feelings in their own way, without pressure, and know there is *HOPE* after a loss. Inside this book you will find resources to: 1) help gauge the feelings of children, 2) help children, as they move forward with day-to-day life, express their emotions with coloring, writing, talking, playing, praying, and loving interactions with you.

Months after Abby died, Ashlin scribbled this story onto the same legal pad we had used months before to circle her feelings. She expressed beautifully, in the simple words of an 8-year-old, how to help other kids through their grief. And so, *The Story of Hope* was born.

Melinda

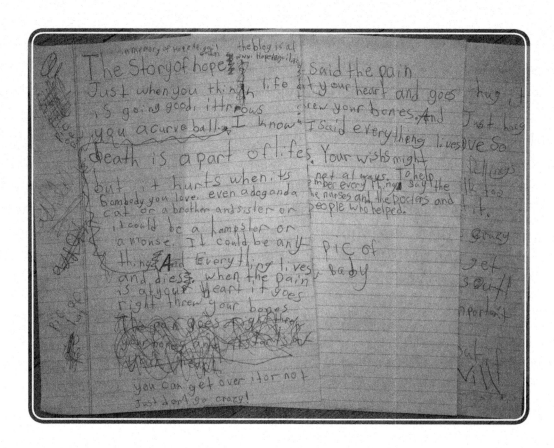

My name is Ashlin and I am 8 years old. My little sister, Hope Abigail "Abby," was born with Trisomy 18. She was very sick and only lived 12 days. I loved my sister so much and miss her every day.

Just when you think life is going well, it throws you a curveball.

Everyone lives and dies. I know death is a part of life, but it hurts when somebody you love dies. It could be a dog or a cat, or even a hamster or a mouse. It hurts so much more, though, when it's your brother or sister.

You might wish things could be different. Sometimes your wish and prayer will come true, but sometimes God has a better plan. You just have to trust Him.

When the pain is in your heart, you can feel it everywhere in your body. You can even feel the pain right through your bones.

It's okay to feel sad, mad, or scared. You have to let your feelings out or else the pain will make you feel worse. It helped for me to hug my dog and my stuffed animal. If you have a pet, hug it as often as you can. If you don't have a pet, hug something you love, like a stuffed animal or a favorite blanket.

Me holding the stuffed animal I took to the hospital when my sister was born.

t helps to talk, too. I talked to my parents and my grandparents, even my cousin. Somedays I wanted to talk about how I felt. Others days I didn't know what to say, so I drew a picture.

I feel . . .

t's OK if you don't know what to say or the words to use to explain how you feel. You can use the pages in this book to draw, color, write, or circle the way you are feeling. It's easy. And don't be afraid to ask for help if you need it.

Let's get started!

QUICK COACHING TIPS FOR PARENTS/CAREGIVERS

As children adjust to the loss, the use of this book and other resources will be needed less and less. Your child can point to, circle, or talk about the expression on the emotion scale that best fits them on a particular day. Or they can use the boy/girl blank face to draw the emotion. Copies can be made to use as often as needed. The coloring pages include open-ended questions to prompt discussion, and can be used at any time or as often as needed.

When or if your child expresses sadness:

♥ Ask if there is anything they need or that you can do to help.

♥ Ask if they have any questions. Many times, the same questions will be asked over and over. Be patient. As their understanding of the loss progresses, the frequency of questions will fade as well.

♥ When the vocabulary and maturity doesn't exist to express feelings with words, playing a favorite game or coloring together often provides a comfort level where emotions flow more freely. Have them choose a picture from the book to color together, and ask why they chose it. This will open up further communication.

Based on our experience, here are a few points to remember:

- ♥ Kids grieve differently from adults. There is no right or wrong way and there is no time limit to grief.

- ♥ Kids are resiliant, but though they may appear indifferent, their grief and pain can show up in other ways, such as extreme aggravation with homework, short temper with friends and family, intense reactions to small frustrations, etc.

- ♥ Finding a keepsake item and making a memory box is a great activity that offers many opportunities for future discussions.

TODAY, I FEEL...

Point to, circle, or talk about which emotion best fits you today.

TODAY, I FEEL...

Use the boy or girl face to draw the way you are feeling today.

What is your favorite memory of _____ (brother or sister)?

_____

What do you miss most about _____?

_____

What is your favorite activity to do with your family?

_____

_____

What does your favorite picture of _____show?

_____

Share your favorite story about _____.

You can write it down or tell someone you love.

What did you love most about _____?

_____

Who are your best friends? What do you love most about them?

_____

What does this picture make you think of? A fishing trip?

A swimming experience under water? An aquarium you saw on vacation?

_____

Do you have a favorite activity that reminds you of _____?

_____

Think of your most favorite place you went with _____.

Did you go on a train, in a bus or car, or on an airplane?

After Abby died, I wrote this poem about her. As you begin to feel better, maybe you, too, can write about the loved one you lost.

HOPE ABIGAIL

One day a tiny baby came to the earth
She was 3 pounds, 5 ounces.
Her outsides were perfect, but her insides were not.
She was a little angel. She was a bundle of pink.
Wrapped fingers and little toes, she was a present from God,
with a small little head and a name as beautiful as Hope.
She got tired and her little body gave out,
but before it gave out her heartbeat was strong.
She smiled at me when I spoke and I will never forget it.
Everybody looked at her website … she was famous!
God gave us a darling Hope.
Sugar and spice and everything nice, tiny fingers, tiny toes, the love of my life.
You gave us joy. You're a prayer from God.
We love you, Hope, and you will always be my sister!

CONTACT INFORMATION

To order additional copies of this book, please visit

www.redemption-press.com.

Also available on Amazon.com and BarnesandNoble.com

Or by calling toll free 1-844-2REDEEM.

CPSIA information can be obtained
at www.ICGtesting.com
Printed in the USA
BVOW03s0228110317
478357BV00008B/23/P